Restart: Revised

A Journey to Becoming Debt-Free

Kim Angela Lee

RESTART! REVISED
A JOURNEY TO
BECOMING DEBT-FREE

KIM ANGELA LEE

Restart!: Revised

A JOURNEY TO BE DEBT-FREE

Kim Angela Lee

Published by "Nickels and Dimes Solutions, L.L.C."

Printed in the United States of America

© United States Copyright 2021

No. 1-10373012001

ISBN: 978-0578873558

TABLE OF CONTENT

DEDICATION

I dedicate this book to my children
Joseph and Gabrielle, their
children, and generations to come.

With tremendous gratitude, I thank my parents
Frankie, John, Michelle, and my sister.
Kari for her love and faith in me and the
adventures of my life.
I honor my pastors Calvin and Cheri Sapp
for your continued support, prayers, and wisdom.

I also dedicate this book to everyone
who believes in me and helped push
me toward my purpose.

QUOTES

➤ "It's not about how you begin; it's where you end." ~ K Lee

➤ "If you have no vision of yourself in the future, then you have nothing to live for." ~ Les Brown

➤ "Friendship is born at that moment when one person says to another: 'What! You too? I thought I was the only one." ~ C.S. Lewis

➤ "Nourish the mind like you would the body." ~ Jim Rohn

➤ "The foundation of a fresh financial

start actually has nothing to do with money or specific financial do's and don'ts." ~ Suze Orman

➤ "Failure is the opportunity to begin again, more intelligently." ~ Henry Ford

➤ "Do not spoil what you have by desiring what you have not." ~ Epicurus

➤ "Victory is sweetest when you've known defeat." ~ Malcolm Forbes

CHAPTER 1

RESTART

Wow! Who would have thought of living a debt-free life and loving it? There are not many other ways to express true financial freedom. Well, that was the end, not the beginning.

Like many young adults, I used to love buying new clothes and splurging on little luxuries, living in the moment without much thought for the future. At 18 years old, I got my first credit card and went on a shopping spree, racking up over $500 in debt. I was shocked to learn that I had to pay the full amount back the next month with no rollover or grace period. I was an 18-year-old gone wild fresh out of the gate. It was quite a hefty sum to spend, and the thought of having to pay it all off the following month was very unsettling, to say the least.

I failed instantly in the finances of real life and hard knocks were knocking at the door of my wallet. I didn't have the financial literacy to recognize that I didn't need a credit card. I believe that every student should have a finance class before leaving high school to ensure their economic success.

FUN-FACT: in 1955, the first U.S. patent was granted containing the phrase "Credit Card."

LET'S TALK ABOUT VISION:

As defined by Merriam-webster.com, vision is a thought, concept, or object formed by the imagination. Vision can also be defined as a method for achieving an end. Either way, you look at it; I did not possess vision when it came down to my last year of high school. I just wanted to graduate, be gone, and never look back. I wish it were that simple. I had my wins and losses in high school. I had initially pursued going straight from high school to the military. However, that pursuit was sidelined by unforeseen circumstances.

Well, it was April, and in two months, I will be honored at my high school graduation. Now I decided I wanted to go to college, why not? My friends were on their way off to college. Not only did I want to go to college, but I wanted to get away. This New York girl started applying to colleges all over the nation. I remember quite a few in Florida and Virginia. As for as late applications were concerned, I definitely had my fair share.

A whopping 90% of my college applications were filed late. I did not score high on the college entrance exams, which became an issue when it came to potential acceptance letters from higher learning institutions.

Through many prayers and God's grace and mercy, I was accepted into a college in Virginia. This was not so bad because I wasn't all alone. Some other high school classmates applied for the same college. They were also accepted to the same college I was fortunate to be accepted in that year. From there, I went off to college with no scholarships, barely any money, and a few student loans that would require my attention in the future. I just was running like a dog without I leash without any clear direction. Just to note, I had an original plan which fell through and unfortunately, I didn't have a backup plan.

A backup plan would have been quite handy in determining a path to my future. There I went with loans consisting of a first-semester student loan and a second-semester student loan. I often thought to myself, "Where does it end"?

I knew I didn't want to be in a bunch of debt, but those loans were the only way that I could even consider going to college. By the way, I didn't finish college, like many other college students. Over 50% of new students with the burden of college loans do not finish college.

However, I did have another route to try to have my college tuition paid for. I joined the Armed Forces of the United States of America to take advantage of the Army G.I. bill.

I wish I had the privilege of reading DEBT-FREE DEGREE by Anthony Oneal. I recommend this book to every person desiring to go to college. This read will change your life.

FUN-FACT:

The Servicemen's Readjustment Act of 1944, commonly known as the G.I. Bill, was a law that provided a range of benefits for returning World War II veterans (commonly referred to as G.I.s). The original G.I. Bill expired in 1956, but the term "G.I. Bill" is still used to refer to programs created to assist U.S. military veterans. (Wikipedia)

A decade later, I faced some formidable life obstacles and elected to move across the country with my children and whatever possessions could fit in our van.

The burden of the student load was ever persistent in my life. No matter where I went, the weight of my debt was always present. It's been a decade, and I still find myself struggling with my student loans.

As the saying goes, "You can run, but you can't hide" - a lesson that still resonates with me today.

CHAPTER 2

NOTHING TO FEAR BUT FEAR

Many have given the word fear an acronym. F.E.A.R. is an acronym for False Evidence Appearing Real.

Let me tell you, my debt was a very real and daunting experience. Have you ever avoided answering the phone because you thought it might be a bill collector? I'm sure you have. Or perhaps you've dreaded seeing a "past due" or "last notice" bill arrive in the mail, red lettering, and all? Yes, it's a frightening experience – one that I can personally attest to.

The fear of not being able to provide food for your family can be paralyzing. Unfortunately, I've been there before. And the thought of the government garnishing your wages or having your car repossessed due to missed payments can be overwhelming, leading to desperate measures like hiding your car a few blocks away. These experiences are not only heart-wrenching but also cause immense fear and anxiety.

Personal trainer and author Dax Moy provides an alternative definition for the acronym F.E.A.R.: Forever Expecting Awful Results. This differs significantly from the previous definition I have been familiar with for years. It's enough to make me want to give up and stop striving for success.

It all comes down to shifting your mindset. Instead of dreading the worst, try accepting good results. Have you ever heard of F.E.A.R. - Forever Expecting Awful Results? It's time to let go of that mentality and embrace positivity!

Reframing Negative Outcomes for Positive Change may sound counterintuitive, but accepting negative outcomes is not about settling for less.

It's about recognizing the reality of the situation and using it as fuel to create positive change.

Instead of expecting awful results, acknowledge the possibility of negative outcomes while maintaining hope for a better future. A shift in perspective is needed, not just on an individual level, but within families, societies, and even nations. Let's work together to create a better world.

Are you feeling stuck and unsure about the future? The first step towards change is shifting your mindset. Remember that things won't be like this forever. It's up to you to make a change and take small steps toward a more positive outlook. Don't be afraid to face your fears and take a different direction. Start by focusing on the good and taking small steps forward. You have the power to turn past results into new opportunities. With a fresh perspective, you can strive for a better future and make progress toward your goals.

Have you ever experienced the fear of losing your job and being uncertain of your eligibility for an unemployment check? Or the disappointment when you don't receive a stimulus check? Imagine the distress of returning home to find that the electricity has been turned off on a hot summer day. Don't let fear hold you back – turn the page and welcome the next chapter of your life!

How do we override that? If you have been the recipient of these horrible fears, then it is time to take steps of faith to a better tomorrow.

It's time to become financially literate and live the life you have been dreaming about. Perhaps blind faith, or how about trust or even courage?

FUN FACT: The Philadelphia Stock Exchange was the first official U.S. securities exchange, formed in 1790- Investopedia.

CHAPTER 3

COURAGE YOU CAN RELY ON

Let's talk about courage. Precisely what is courage? One definition of courage is the ability to do something that frightens one. "What if we had the courage to try something new?

By adopting a new perspective on debt, you can unlock new opportunities for growth.

It's time to change the way you perceive debt. Instead of relying on credit cards to get through the next pay cycle, let's seek out alternatives. How about we muster up the courage to say no to payday loans? These types of loans can put you in a debt spiral faster than anything else. It's best to leave them alone and explore other options.

One alternative to payday loans is to consider borrowing from friends or family. You may feel hesitant to do so, but having an open and honest conversation about your financial situation can help you receive the support you need without the high-interest rates of a payday loan.

It's important to also take a closer look at your spending habits and find ways to cut back on expenses. This can help you free up some cash to put towards paying off any existing debt. Creating a budget and sticking to it can also help you stay on track and avoid accumulating more debt.

The debt cycle and stronghold can only get more in-depth with this scheme of a loan. You will never get ahead. On a lighter note, maybe we can get creative and learn how to cook meals at home economically wise and light on the checkbook. Let's do something different to break the stranglehold of the debt cycle.

Write down everything you owe on paper and begin to face these fears with courage.

It is time for an upgrade mindset exchange. Let's do things on purpose, and let's start with a plan.

Maybe we can sell some stuff, or how about starting a new family tradition of cutting up your credit cards? I know it sounds far-fetched, but drastic times call for drastic measures.

If you ever want to experience true freedom from credit card debt, then cut them up!

Remember, changing your point of view about debt is not an overnight process, but taking small steps toward financial responsibility can make a big difference in the long run.

By exploring alternatives to payday loans and making conscious efforts to manage your finances, you can start to feel more in control of your financial situation.

FUN FACT: In 1865, the Secret Service was created to suppress widespread counterfeiting- secretservice.gov.

CHAPTER 4

DISCIPLINE EQUALS SUCCESS

The Power of Discipline in Achieving a Debt-Free Lifestyle:

For many, the dream of living debt-free remains elusive. However, it's achievable with discipline. Discipline refers to the process of training or developing oneself through instruction and exercise, particularly in self-control. Needless to say, self-control is a potent tool in this pursuit.

Self-control is the ability to manage one's impulses, emotions, or desires. How does this relate to the pursuit of becoming debt-free? It's crucial and requires discipline. Acquiring everything that catches your eye is not a wise decision. You must differentiate between your needs and wants, the immediate and delayed, in order to achieve fiscal responsibility.

You have to put sincere thoughts into the decisions that you make. The decisions you make now will affect you later on in whatever process or whatever journey you are embarking on.

The Importance of Discipline in Various Aspects of Life:

Let's talk about discipline. It's a vital factor in many aspects of our lives. Eating habits, for instance, require discipline to avoid potential health problems, such as obesity or malnutrition.

Similarly, financial discipline is crucial to prevent overspending or draining savings before emergencies arise. Without discipline, the outcome is often a lack of emergency funds or inadequate savings for the future.

It's essential to maintain moderation and not indulge in reckless behavior indefinitely.

We can't live on the uncontrolled wild side for the rest of our lives.

Do you long for financial freedom? Remember, it all starts with you! Achieving financial independence is a personal endeavor that only you can undertake.

Change is never easy, but it all starts with a strong desire to make a difference for yourself and future generations. Take things one step at a time and you'll start to see progress. By shifting your perspective on finance, you have the power to pave the way for a brighter future.

You have to want change to happen. It is not easy; however, you have to want it first for you and those who come after you. Change begins one step and a time.

You can change your generation by making a change in how you view your finances.

TIME TO REFOCUS AND STAY ON TRACK:

It's important to realign, adapt and keep your goals in sight. Beware! Appearances can be deceiving. What you perceive and long for may sometimes lead you to a financial knockout.

ACHIEVING FINANCIAL FREEDOM THROUGH REASSESSMENT AND HARD WORK:

It's common for our financial issues to stem from planning oversights. Often, we're simply trying to keep up with our peers.

It's crucial to reassess and redirect our focus toward financial independence. Determination and hard work are the keys to achieving this goal.

FUN FACT: Lizzie Magie was the visionary of Monopoly, known initially as the "Landlord's Game." - Smithsonian Magazine

CHAPTER 5

DETERMINATION DETERMINES YOUR DESTINY

What Does Determination Mean to You?

Determination can have various meanings for different people.

Take a moment to reflect on a past experience where you had to be determined.

This might have involved meeting a goal, adhering to a deadline, or preparing for a significant event. It could be anything from wanting to lose weight to running a full marathon.

THE IMPORTANCE OF DETERMINATION:

Determination is the driving force behind success. However, determination can manifest differently for each individual, depending on their goals and aspirations. It's important to remain adaptable because success is not a one-size-fits-all solution.

ACHIEVING YOUR GOALS: THE IMPORTANCE OF FOCUS, PLANNING, AND VISION:

When there's something you really want, you'll do whatever it takes to get it – even if it means moving heaven and earth. However, it's crucial to focus your efforts and develop a plan of action to achieve your goals.

Writing down your plan, setting goals, envisioning the end result, and having a clear vision of success are critical components of success. Remember, anything is possible with the right mindset and approach.

My Suggestion: Put Your Plan on Paper. Would you mind considering writing down your plan on a piece of paper? You could even cut out a picture from a magazine to place on your wall and say, "That's my goal." Visualize that dream home, the car you want, and maybe even those skinny jeans.

THE POWER OF DETERMINATION:

When you have a clear goal in front of you and a strong determination to achieve it, you can go a long way. Determination can accelerate your progress and make even the toughest tasks seem achievable. It helps you overcome obstacles and inspires those around you. When you feel like you can't go on, determination gives you the extra push you need to keep moving forward.

Imagine Yourself in a Marathon: Pushing Past Pain to Victory. Let me describe the 18th mile of a marathon – it feels like running into a wall. But with determination,

I pushed through the tightness caused by lactic acid, the weariness, and the pain. My only goal was to reach the finish line, and I did.

Despite the 26.2-mile course that many thought I could not defeat, I persevered. The weeks of hard training paid off, and I am now the proud owner of a medal. Right now, I can't help but pat myself on the back.

Recently, I had a conversation with one of my beta testers. I had previously reminded her about the start of a new month and a new budget. She was thrilled that her budget was complete and found it easier with each iteration.

However, she did have some questions and asked for guidance about some decisions regarding her future.

ENCOURAGING A FRIEND TO EXPLORE HOMEOWNERSHIP OPTIONS:

A friend confided in me that she had spoken with a realtor to explore her options as a homeowner. Having retired a year ago, she hadn't given much thought to this decision until now. I urged her to look into different options, including the types of properties she might be interested in, how many rooms and bathrooms she would need, and more. I even suggested that she visit various websites to see what's available.

My intention was simply to encourage her to explore her options without any pressure or obligation.

As the day came to a close, she inquired about my home, and I was delighted to share that I paid off my house in under 20 years. My goal was to be mortgage-free by the time I turned 50.

Despite consuming a steady diet of rice and beans, I achieved my objective. To celebrate, I had a mortgage-burning party.

My determination to succeed was unwavering. I had a clear goal in sight and was determined to achieve it no matter what. I took on extra work, sold some of my belongings, and worked tirelessly to make it happen. And I did! I met my goal well before the deadline and I couldn't be more thrilled. Now that I am in a position to help others, I am committed to being a better listener and giver.

With self-motivation and hard work, reaching your goals is possible. Having others to support and motivate you is great, but many debt-free people have learned to rely on self-encouragement.

FUN FACT: In 1914, the Bureau of Internal Revenue released the first income tax form, Form 1040.

CHAPTER 6

A COMPELLING REASON TO WANT CHANGE

It's time to break the cycle and become a generational agent of change.

What motivates us to make a change in our lives?

Why would anyone want to go through the hassle, heartache, or headache of breaking a cycle?

The answer lies in our desire to escape the monotony of everyday life. Often, we are trapped in a cycle of generational debt, illness, and bad habits that seem impossible to overcome. But it is up to us to become the agents of change and break these cycles for good.

Imagine being proud of the legacy you create for future generations. If you want to make a difference, it has to start with you.

What will you do today to begin this process?

Why not take the first step towards becoming a wealth builder, leading your generation out of debt?

Although the journey may not be easy, it will be worth it in the end. Remember, slow progress is still progress - so take that first step and begin to break the cycle.

Breaking the cycle and becoming an agent of change can be a daunting task, but the benefits of doing so are immeasurable. Here are some additional thoughts to consider as you embark on this journey:

Recognize that breaking the cycle is not just about personal gain. It is also about creating a better future for those who come after you.

By breaking the cycle of generational debt, illness, and bad habits, you are paving the way for a brighter future for your children and grandchildren.

START SMALL: Breaking the cycle doesn't happen overnight. It's important to set realistic goals and take small steps toward achieving them. Celebrate your progress along the way to keep yourself motivated.

Seek support from others. Breaking the cycle is not something you have to do alone. Surround yourself with people who support your goals and can help you stay accountable.

Be patient and persistent. Breaking the cycle can be a long and challenging process. Don't get discouraged if you hit roadblocks along the way. Remember that slow progress is still progress, and each step you take is bringing you closer to your goal.

Remember, becoming an agent of change requires courage, determination, and a willingness to challenge the status quo. But by taking that first step towards breaking the cycle, you are already on your way to creating a better future for yourself and your loved ones.

CHAPTER 7

DO NOT DEVALUE YOURSELF

BELIEVE IN YOURSELF AND KEEP MOVING FORWARD:

"I can't" and "It's too hard" are phrases that connote failure and discouragement, while "I have never done it this way before" reveals fear and timidity. It's essential to realize your potential and believe in yourself. The power lies within you, and you must take the first step and press forward. Learning from the mistakes and successes of others is a valuable resource. Consider picking up a book to gain insight into the subject matter and enhance your knowledge.

As a financial coach, I am passionate about investing in the financial literacy of others to help them develop into great navigators of their own destinies. Empowering people with the wisdom and knowledge of understanding their hard-earned money excites me. I am thrilled to see individuals achieve their goals and experience freedom concerning their finances. Watching people grow and discover new opportunities is what makes my job fulfilling.

INTERVIEWS ON FINANCIAL LITERACY: MARRIED COUPLES AND HIGH SCHOOL STUDENTS

Average Married Couple:

- Budgeting: Leave it to my spouse due to their administrative strengths. Know your strengths and weaknesses.
- Credit Cards: Highest amount ever had was three.
- College: Attended through loans and credit cards.
- Financial Literacy: Started understanding finances in their 30s.
- Spouse: Was a saver before and after marriage.

- Debt: Knew the spouse's debt amount before marriage, which was not much.
- Wedding: Did not go into debt, received help from parents, and planned.
- Savings: The goal is to save more and spend less.
- College for Kids: Plan to help out and hope for scholarships or help from grandparents.

High School Student:

- College: Not sure which one to attend, but many colleges want them from GA to CA.
- Major: Wanted to study video game design, but now interested in writing.
- College vs. Trade School: Plans to attend college.
- College Duration: Does not know if they will attend a two-year or four-year college.

- Paying for College: Plans to get scholarships and is focusing on getting good grades.
- SATs: Has not taken them yet.
- College Location: Not sure whether to stay in-state or go out-of-state.
- Working While Attending College: Has not thought about it.

As a gift, the book "Debt Free Degree" by Anthony Oneal is recommended to the high school student to encourage them to plan for their future and avoid the burden of student loans.

Fun Fact: Only 8% of the world currency is physical cash.

CHAPTER 8

INVEST IN YOURSELF

Investing in yourself means believing in your potential and taking intentional actions to learn, grow, and create value. It requires prioritizing self-improvement and making sacrifices, like saying "no" to certain activities or expenses that don't align with your goals. To achieve financial freedom, for instance, you may need to forgo certain luxuries and invest in your financial literacy instead.

Small steps can lead to significant progress. Reading a financial literacy book for 15 minutes a day, for example, can help you gain knowledge and confidence in managing your finances. Seeking the help of a coach can also provide guidance and support as you work towards your goals.

Change can be challenging, but it is necessary to achieve a different outcome in life. Take inspiration from babies who learn to walk by falling and getting back up again. Encourage yourself and be your own cheerleader. Visualize your goals, claim them, and take action toward them.

Similarly, you can learn from your mistakes and keep moving forward toward your goals.

FUN FACT: did you know that Martha Washington was the first and only woman to appear on U.S. paper currency?

Her image was discontinued in 1957, but it's interesting to learn about the history of our currency and the women who have made significant contributions throughout history.

CHAPTER 9

STEPS

These are all great steps to help you on your journey to financial freedom! I can provide some additional context and elaboration on each of these steps to help you get started.

1. Emergency fund $1000: This is a crucial step in achieving financial freedom. Having an emergency fund ensures that you have a safety net in case of unexpected expenses. Start by setting aside $1000 in a separate savings account that is easily accessible in case of an emergency.

2. Budget: Creating a budget is an essential step towards financial freedom. It helps you track your spending habits, identify areas where you can cut back, and plan for your future goals. Start by listing all your monthly income and expenses, and

then create a plan to allocate your money towards your financial goals.

3. Use Cash: Paying with cash instead of credit cards can help you avoid overspending and keep you accountable for your purchases. Try using the envelope method, where you allocate a set amount of cash for each category of expense and only spend what's in the envelope.

4. Spend less: Cutting back on unnecessary expenses is key to achieving financial freedom. Take a hard look at your spending habits and identify areas where you can cut back. This could be as simple as bringing your lunch to work instead of eating out, or canceling subscriptions you don't use.

5. Save More: Saving money is a crucial step towards achieving financial freedom. Look for ways to increase your income, such as taking on a side hustle or negotiating a raise at work.

Then, make a plan to save a portion of your income each month towards your financial goals.

6. **Pay off Debt:** Debt can be a major obstacle to achieving financial freedom. Start by making a list of all your debts and their interest rates. Then, create a plan to pay off your debts starting with the highest interest rate first.

7. **Write Down Goals:** Writing down your financial goals can help you stay focused and motivated on your journey to financial freedom. Be specific about what you want to achieve and create a plan to reach those goals. Remember to celebrate your successes along the way!

CHAPTER 10

GETTING TO THE ROOT OF THE MATTER

Understanding your financial situation is crucial to achieving financial freedom. One way to start is by identifying your spending habits. I call it getting to the root of the matter. This can help you determine why you spend the way you do and how you can make changes to reach your financial goals.

There are different spending personalities, each with its unique characteristics. Identifying which category, you fall into can help you understand your spending habits better.

Are you a spender, savorer, shopper, debtor, or investor?

Once you know your spending personality, you can start making changes to improve your financial situation.

By getting to the root of your spending habits, you can address the underlying issues that may be holding you back. Perhaps you spend money to cope with stress or emotions, or maybe you have a fear of missing out (FOMO) that drives your spending.

Understanding the root cause of a problem is essential in finding a lasting solution. By identifying the source of the issue, you can address it directly, rather than merely trying to manage the symptoms. This approach can help you to avoid repeating the same financial mistakes and can lead to a more profound sense of healing and growth.

Example:

As a child, you may have grown up below the poverty line and experienced extreme lack. However, now that you are an adult, you have no limit on your spending, which has resulted in significant debt.

It can be difficult to break free from the cycle of financial struggle that you may have experienced growing up. However, it's important to recognize that your current financial situation is within your control and there are steps you can take to improve it

Whatever the reason, understanding it can help you develop healthier financial habits and work towards financial freedom.

Getting to the root of a problem can be a challenging process, but the rewards are worth it in the end. By addressing the underlying issues, you can experience greater freedom and a more fulfilling life.

As you embark on your journey to financial freedom and healing, don't hesitate to seek assistance when needed.

It's perfectly acceptable to ask for help along the way.

CHAPTER 11

EVERYDAY FINANCIAL AFFIRMATIONS

Affirmations for Financial Abundance:

- I consistently earn more than I spend
- My bank accounts remain positive
- My financial needs are met daily, weekly, and monthly
- I experience unforeseen income growth
- My money is growing through dividends and interest
- I regularly receive raises and bonuses
- I am continuously improving my financial knowledge and wisdom
- I am debt-free, and my needs are fulfilled
- Wealth is constantly flowing into my life
- My financial choices are wise and fruitful
- I am prosperous and abundant
- I am a wealth creator

- I am prepared for the future
- I am in control of my life and finances
- My bills are always paid on time
- Opportunities for financial growth come to me daily
- My financial decisions will positively impact future generations
- I am building a lasting legacy for my family
- I am a problem solver, and people seek my financial advice
- I am financially free and can give generously
- I am creating a legacy of wealth and success for generations to come
- I am passionate about achieving financial freedom.

MEET THE AUTHOR

Kim is a Ramsey Financial Coach Master Training graduate, having coordinated multiple financial classes and workshops over the years.

Her signature speech "Getting to the Root of the Matter" is a testament to her expertise.

Kim is the founder of Nickels & Dimes Solutions L.L.C., and she derives immense pleasure from imparting wisdom and knowledge to others.

As a mother of two and grandmother of six, she is passionate about empowering people.

Kim has been a guest on SHIFT TV, and she is also the author of two books, "Restart- A Journey to Becoming Debt-Free" and "Rediscover Your Voice," both available on Amazon.

CONTACT

Follow me on:

Website:

https://nickelsandimesolutions.com/

At Linked-In

https://www.linkedin.com/in/kim-angela-lee/

www.ingramcontent.com/pod-product-compliance
Lightning Source LLC
Chambersburg PA
CBHW071326200326
41520CB00013B/2878